Christopher Columbus

A Proud Heritage The Hispanic Library

Christopher Columbus

Opening the Americas to European Exploration

Michael Burgan

The Child's World®

Published in the United States of America by The Child's World®
PO Box 326 • Chanhassen, MN 55317-0326 • 800-599-READ • www.childsworld.com

Acknowledgments
   The Childs World®: Mary Berendes, Publishing Director
   Editorial Directions, Inc.: E. Russell Primm, Editorial Director; Pam Rosenberg, Project Editor;
   Melissa McDaniel, Line Editor; Katie Marsico, Assistant Editor; Matt Messbarger, Editorial
   Assistant; Susan Hindman, Copyeditor; Susan Ashley and Sarah E. De Capua, Proofreaders;
   Chris Simms and Olivia Nellums, Fact Checkers; Timothy Griffin/IndexServ, Indexer; Cian
   Loughlin O'Day and Dawn Friedman, Photo Researchers; Linda S. Koutris, Photo Selector
   Creative Spark: Mary Francis and Rob Court, Design and Page Production
   Cartography by XNR Productions, Inc.

Photos
   Cover: Detail from *Christopher Columbus* by Jose Roldan
   Cover photograph: Archivo Iconografico, S.A./Corbis
   Interior photographs: The Art Archive: 9 (Album/Joseph Martin), 16 (Mireille Vautier); The
   Art Archive/Dagli Orti: 7 (Christopher Columbus Birthplace Valladolid), 23 (Museo de la
   Torre del Oro, Seville); Bettmann/Corbis: 13, 32; Getty Images: 11 (Roger Viollet), 19
   (Hulton | Archive); Historical Picture Archive/Corbis: 8, 21; North Wind Picture Archive: 15,
   18, 24, 27, 33, 35; Orban Thierry/Corbis Sygma: 30.

Library of Congress Cataloging-in-Publication Data
   Cataloging-in-Publication data for this title has been applied for and is available from the
   United States Library of Congress.

One	A Great and Mysterious Explorer	6
Two	The Voyage West	14
Three	Triumph and Troubles	22
Four	Last Voyages	30
	Timeline	36
	Glossary	38
	Further Information	39
	Index	40

Chapter One

A Great and Mysterious Explorer

In 1492, Christopher Columbus made a daring voyage across the Atlantic Ocean. He was convinced that he could sail west from Spain and reach the rich lands of China, Japan, and India. Before him, no one had ever tried to make this trip. Always confident, Columbus hoped to gain vast wealth and power by discovering a new sea route to Asia.

Columbus, however, did not reach his goal. Blocking his path was a huge landmass—the continents of North and South America. Before Columbus's voyage, Europeans did not realize that the Americas sat to the west between their continent and Asia. They also did not know about the people who lived there. Thinking he had reached what Europeans called the Indies, Columbus named these original Americans "Indians."

In one sense, Columbus was a failure. He did not reach Asia by sailing west, as he had hoped. He also faced many difficulties on his later trips to the Americas He never found the huge quantities of gold he sought, and he died almost forgotten by people who once praised him.

Yet in other ways, Columbus was the greatest explorer of all time. He spent years planning for that

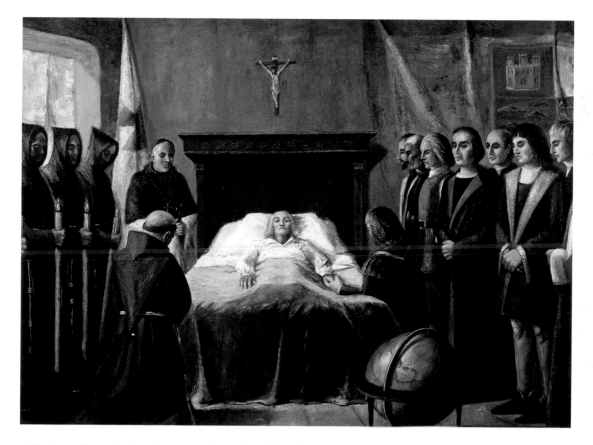

Christopher Columbus on his deathbed. Today, he is honored as the explorer who opened the Americas to European exploration but at the time of his death, many people considered him a failure.

Columbus studies charts and maps in preparation for the voyage. His historic voyage took many years of planning.

first voyage. He never gave up when several leaders refused to pay for his first voyage. And he showed remarkable bravery, sailing far beyond the known lands of the time. His journeys helped Spain acquire colonies and wealth. Other European countries then followed the Spanish to the Americas, setting up their own colonies. More explorers crossed the Atlantic, looking for new sea routes and territory. Europeans settled in North and South America, bringing their art, religions, and political ideas.

Columbus's voyages also had a tremendous impact on millions of Native Americans and Africans—usually for the worse. The Europeans took the Native Americans' land and forced them into slavery. The Europeans also spread diseases previously unknown in North and South America, killing many Native Americans. Needing new workers for their farms and mines, the Europeans turned to Africa, buying slaves there and bringing them to the Americas.

Columbus, like other explorers of his time, did not worry about the fact that people were already living in the Americas when he claimed the land for Spain.

Today, some people praise Columbus for his explorations. Others blame him for the suffering many people endured after Europeans began to dominate North and South America. One thing, however, is clear—with his voyages to the Americas, Columbus changed world history.

Who Was Columbus?

Hundreds of books have been written about Columbus and his explorations, yet in some ways no one knows the complete truth about him and his life. His son Hernando wrote a biography of Columbus. He said that his father "was not without some mysteries."

Columbus seemed to prefer that people not know all the details about his early years, perhaps because he came from a poor background. Even what he looked like is a mystery, because no one ever drew or painted him while he was alive. From written descriptions, however, we know he had red hair that turned white at an early age, and he was taller than most men of the era.

Some historians have claimed that Christopher Columbus (or Cristoforo Colombo, in Italian) was not the explorer's real name. He may have been abandoned as a child and taken that name later on. Others claim he was not Italian, though most historians accept that he was. A few people suggest he was Jewish and his family **converted** to Roman Catholicism, the Christian religion of Italy at the time. Other details of his early years may be myths. Most biographies, for example, describe how the young Columbus survived a shipwreck and came ashore in Portugal. At least one historian, however, says this thrilling episode may not have occurred.

Despite the questions and claims, most historians do accept some basic details of Columbus's life. He was born in 1451 in Genoa, Italy, a thriving port filled with rich merchants. Columbus's father, however, was a wool weaver who never made much money. As a boy, Columbus probably spent time working in his father's shop. He received little schooling, but over the years he taught himself about

Young Christopher Columbus studied geography and other subjects on his own. Though he had little formal schooling, he had a great desire to explore the world beyond his hometown of Genoa.

geography and other subjects. His studies fueled his desire to explore the world.

When he was about 14, Columbus took his first job on a ship. Genoa was famous for its sailors, and its ships crossed the Mediterranean Sea and sometimes sailed north to England. Genoese sailors also worked on foreign ships. Before Columbus was born, Portugal had opened a new era of trade and exploration. The Portuguese made the first European voyages to western Africa, and they discovered islands close to Europe in the Atlantic Ocean.

About 1476, Columbus ended up in Lisbon, the capital of Portugal. Columbus's younger brother Bartolomeo was a **cartographer** there. He may have helped Columbus settle in his new home. Within a year, however, Columbus was back at sea. During his travels, Columbus learned about the currents and winds that helped ships sail the Atlantic Ocean. He also heard sailors' tales about distant lands. And Columbus heard the theories of a famous Italian geographer, Paolo Toscanelli. The geographer suggested that the distance between Europe and China was not that large, and ships could sail west from Europe to reach Asia. Columbus did more research on this idea. Slowly, the plan for his historic voyage began to take shape.

For several centuries, most people accepted the idea that Christopher Columbus was the first European to reach North or South America. In Iceland, however, people told tales about an earlier Atlantic explorer who had sailed west

and found new lands. About the year 1000, the stories went, Leif Eriksson sailed from Greenland and discovered a land he called Vinland. The **Norse** explorer set up a small camp there, and other settlers followed him. The threat of attack from the native people, however, eventually forced the Norse back to Greenland.

Over time, many people debated where Vinland was located or if it existed at all. In 1960, Norwegian explorer and scientist Helge Ingstad settled the question when he found the remains of a Norse village in Newfoundland, Canada. Today, Leif Eriksson rightly receives credit for reaching the Americas more than 400 years before Columbus was born.

Chapter Two

The Voyage West

About 1484, Christopher Columbus met with King John II of Portugal. He explained to the king his plan for sailing west to Asia. King John and his advisors dismissed Columbus's claims that he could find a new route to the East. The Portuguese hoped to reach the Indies by sailing south around Africa. Then, they would trade for the spices and other valuable goods found in that region.

After this setback, Columbus left Portugal and headed to Spain. He continued studying geography and sharpening his plan for exploration. In 1486, he tried once again to win government support. He met with Ferdinand and Isabella, the king and queen of Spain. The two rulers chose scholars to study Columbus's plan. The scholars argued that the distance between Europe and Asia was much greater than Columbus believed. His trip west could never succeed, because Spanish ships could not

Columbus presents the plans for his voyage to a group of scholars at Salamanca, Spain, in 1486. Columbus waited several years for this council, appointed by Queen Isabella and King Ferdinand, to make their final recommendation. Unfortunately, they decided that Spain should not finance his voyage.

carry enough supplies for the long voyage. In addition, Spain at the time was battling the **Moors,** who controlled part of southern Spain. Ferdinand and Isabella were focusing their attention—and money—on winning that war. Like King John of Portugal, the Spanish rulers refused to help Columbus.

Sure of his plan, Columbus refused to give up. He tried again to win support from Portugal, but was unsuccessful. Finally, early in 1492, Columbus met again with

Columbus meets with Ferdinand and Isabella. In 1492, he finally convinced the king and queen to support his voyage in search of a quicker route to Asia.

Ferdinand and Isabella. The Spanish army had just defeated the Moors, and the country was united and at peace. Still, the two rulers hesitated to support Columbus.

Making a Deal

Ferdinand and Isabella turned him down again, but Columbus continued trying. He finally convinced the queen that his mission would help spread Catholicism and honor God. Columbus said that she and her husband would also receive most of the riches he might find. In addition to giving him money, Isabella and Ferdinand agreed to make Columbus **viceroy** of the lands he found and claimed for Spain. The explorer would also receive 10 percent of the profits from "all and every kind of merchandise, whether pearls, precious stones, gold, silver [and] spices" found through his efforts.

The Spanish government arranged for Columbus to receive two ships, the *Niña* and the *Pinta*. Known as caravels, these small ships were among the fastest vessels of the day. Columbus then acquired a third ship, the *Santa María*. It was larger and slower than the other two. Columbus chose the *Santa María* as his flagship—the vessel that carries the commander of a naval fleet.

Using money from the royal couple and other investors, Columbus then bought supplies and hired a crew. To captain the *Pinta,* he chose Martín Alonso Pinzón, an experienced Spanish sailor. His brother Vicente Yañez Pinzón commanded the *Niña*. All together, the three ships carried about 90 sailors, mostly Spaniards. Finally, on August 3, 1492, Columbus was ready to sail. As he wrote in his journal, "We proceeded with strong sea winds until the setting of the sun toward the south. . . . "

Mostly Smooth Sailing

The first stop on the trip was the Canary Islands, about 800 miles (1,287 kilometers) southwest of Spain in the Atlantic Ocean. Columbus knew that the winds near the islands would help push his ships westward. While in the Canaries, he took on more supplies and repaired a broken **rudder** on the *Pinta*. On September 6, the small

A ship approaches the Canary Islands. These islands were the first stop for Columbus and his fleet. He restocked his ships there before continuing his voyage. The islands became an important stop for later Spanish expeditions sailing to the Americas.

fleet once again set sail, this time heading west. No one onboard the ships knew when—or if—they would see land again.

The ships cruised the Atlantic without any major problems. "We are all in good spirits," Columbus noted in his journal on September 17. The weather was mostly good, the seas calm, and the sailors stayed healthy.

The Search for Land

After almost two weeks at sea, Martín Pinzón told Columbus he had spotted land. Some of the crew wanted to sail for it, but Columbus said no. He knew they had not gone far enough to reach the Indies. A week later, Pinzón made the same claim. This time, Columbus was ready to head for the shore, but he soon realized that Pinzón had only seen low-lying clouds, not land.

By this time, some of the crew had started to whisper about a **mutiny.** Loyal sailors told Columbus that some of the men were ready to throw him overboard if they did not find land soon. On October 1, after traveling more than 2,000 miles (3,218 km), Columbus wrote that he did not want to frighten the men by telling them how far they had gone since leaving Spain. The sailors had traveled farther across the Atlantic than any other Europeans of that era.

On October 6, the crew saw a welcome sight—land birds flying near the ships. Still, they traveled on for several more days without seeing land. By October 10, the crew once again began to grumble. Columbus told the men that "it was useless to complain; having set out for the Indies I shall continue this voyage until, with God's grace, I reach them." The next day, a carved stick bobbed by the ships, and more land birds flew overhead. The men sensed they were approaching their goal.

During the night of October 11, a sailor on the *Pinta* finally spotted land. Columbus saw it too, and he

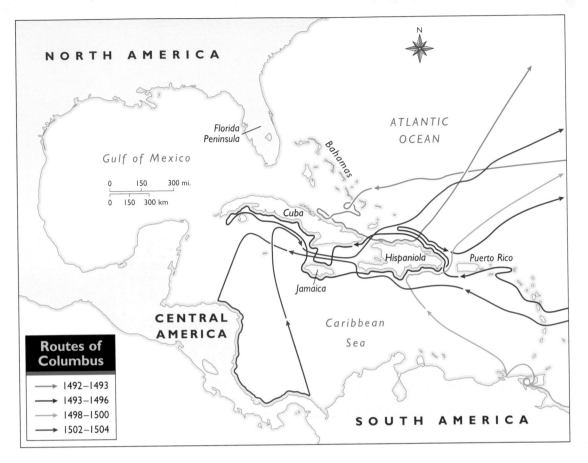

NORTH AMERICA

ATLANTIC OCEAN

Florida Peninsula

Gulf of Mexico

Bahamas

Cuba

Hispaniola

Puerto Rico

Jamaica

CENTRAL AMERICA

Caribbean Sea

SOUTH AMERICA

Routes of Columbus

→ 1492–1493
→ 1493–1496
→ 1498–1500
→ 1502–1504

Columbus sailed to the Americas four times.

ordered the ships to hold their position until the morning. At dawn, Columbus, the other captains, and two officers boarded small boats and went ashore. Columbus claimed the land for Spain. He named it San Salvador—Spanish for "holy savior"—and planted a cross in the sand. All this time, native people on the shore watched the foreigners who now said they owned their homeland. Columbus called these people *Indios*—Indians.

The Native Americans of San Salvador and many neighboring islands were the Taínos. They belonged to a larger group of people called the Arawak. The Taínos had lived in the region for hundreds of years before Columbus arrived. Their original home was most likely South America or Central America. The Taínos followed other Native Americans from those regions who settled on the islands of the Caribbean Sea. Several thousand people might live in a Taíno village.

The Taínos had a formal religion with many different gods. They held religious ceremonies and dances in the center of their villages. The Taínos were ruled by chiefs called caciques. Women were considered the equal of men and could serve as caciques. For food, the Taínos mostly farmed. Their main crops included corn and cassava. The roots of the cassava plant were used to make flour. The Taínos also fished and hunted birds. Their craftspeople made pots, and some skilled workers made jewelry out of gemstones, gold, and shells.

Chapter Three

Triumph and Troubles

Almost as soon as he came ashore, Columbus exchanged presents with the Native Americans who had come out to greet him and his men. The Spanish presented beads and bells, while the Taínos offered cotton, parrots, and other items. The natives, the captain later wrote, were "tall and handsome, their hair not curly, but flowing and thick, like horsehair." The Taínos were friendly and intelligent, and Columbus thought the Spanish could easily make them accept Christianity—one of the goals of his **expedition.** Columbus was deeply religious, and he often said he wanted to honor God with his actions.

Columbus also noticed that some of the Taínos wore gold jewelry. They told him the gold came from a land south of San Salvador. Within a few days, the Spanish set sail again, hoping to find the source of the precious metal. Columbus took seven Taínos with him to bring back to Spain.

Martín Alonzo Pinzón (above), captain of the Pinta, *was one of two brothers who took part in the first voyage of Columbus. His brother, Vicente Yáñez Pinzón, commanded the* Niña. *While Martín is remembered for his disloyalty to Columbus, Vicente stayed with Columbus for the entire expedition.*

For more than a month, the three ships explored the Caribbean Sea. The captain, thinking he had reached Asia, expected to find a large mainland. Instead, he and his crew found a series of islands. Along the way, Columbus recorded the sights, sounds, and smells of the Americas. The sailors were the first Europeans to see the region's manatees and brightly colored fish. Columbus and his crew heard the songs of birds they had never seen before. They smelled flowers from plants unknown in Europe, and Columbus called the smell "the sweetest fragrance in the world."

In late November, Martín Pinzón sailed off on his own in the *Pinta,* leaving Columbus with just two

Columbus was welcomed by the Native Americans on the island of Hispaniola when the Santa Maria *was shipwrecked. Unfortunately, the relationship between the Spanish explorers and the Native Americans worsened over time.*

ships. Columbus was not pleased and assumed Pinzón was interested in finding gold for himself. A month later, the *Santa María* and the *Niña* spent several days at a large island Columbus named Espanola. (Today, it is called Hispaniola, home to the countries of Haiti and the Dominican Republic.) When the ships sailed again, they ran into trouble. The *Santa María* hit coral rocks and began to sink. Columbus and his men escaped the ship and returned to shore, but now the captain had a problem. The *Niña* was too small to carry all the men back to Spain. Columbus decided to build a small fort on Hispaniola and leave 39 men behind. He called the camp La Navidad. Columbus promised to return for them as soon as he could.

On January 4, 1493, Columbus left Hispaniola. Before leaving the Caribbean, his ship met up with the *Pinta*. Columbus was angry that Pinzón had left without permission, but he decided not to punish him. Soon the two ships began their return voyage across the Atlantic. By this time, Columbus knew he had not reached China or Japan, as he had hoped. Earlier explorers, such as Marco Polo, had clearly described the large cities and wealth there. Still, Columbus was sure he had reached the Indies.

Hero's Welcome

Columbus faced several problems on the trip back to Spain. His ships ran into a powerful storm, and the *Niña* and the *Pinta* were separated once again. In late February, Columbus reached the Azores, Portuguese islands about 1,000 miles (1,600 km) from the mainland of Europe. The Portuguese arrested some of the Spanish sailors, supposedly under the orders of King John II. Columbus then sailed on, and in a few weeks another storm forced him to seek safety in Lisbon, Portugal.

The city's residents came out to see the ship and the Indians onboard. Columbus wrote that the Portuguese were "all expressing amazement and praising God" for his successful trip to the Indies. After a brief visit with King John II, Columbus was allowed to sail to Spain. On March 15, the *Niña* returned to its home port of Palos. Soon the *Pinta* followed it into the harbor.

Columbus traveled to Barcelona, where Ferdinand and Isabella were staying. The two rulers had already heard about his success in the Indies. As the captain approached the city, Spaniards ran into the streets. They wanted to see the Indians and greet their new hero. Ferdinand and Isabella gave Columbus all the honors they had promised him, as well as 10,000 gold coins. The rulers said they appreciated "the risk and danger to which you have exposed yourself for our service."

Columbus was already planning his next voyage to land he believed to be the Indies. This time, his goal was to start a Spanish colony, as well as look for new lands and gold. Ferdinand and Isabella gave him 17 ships, and about 1,200 settlers joined the expedition. They included priests and farmers. Columbus promised them plenty of gold and a good life in the Americas.

A Difficult Return

Despite some rough weather along the way, the ships crossed the Atlantic in just over 20 days. After visiting several Caribbean islands, Columbus led his fleet to Hispaniola and the small fort at La Navidad. To his shock, Columbus found that his men had been killed by a nearby Taíno tribe. The Spanish had apparently raided villages and forced local women to live with them. One group of Indians fought back, though some friendly Taínos tried to defend the Spanish.

Members of the Taíno tribe kill the Spanish settlers at La Navidad. The Native Americans were angered by the Spaniards who raided their village and forced some Taíno women to live with them.

Columbus left La Navidad and sailed east, looking for a new site on Hispaniola to build a town. He picked a spot he named La Isabela, for the Spanish queen. The settlers built small huts to live in, a church, a fort, and several small stone buildings. Columbus thought the settlers would find gold not far from their new town. They found some, but not the large amounts they hoped for.

Columbus soon faced several problems. Early in 1494, he had to send more than half his ships back to Spain to get supplies for the settlers. He also tried to assert his power over the hidalgos who had made the trip. These Spanish noblemen wanted to do things their own way and not follow the orders of a foreigner. In addition, Columbus had to deal with the Taínos, who sometimes stole from the Spanish or threatened the settlement. The relationship between the two peoples worsened, leading to war. Columbus wrote, "Our men won such a victory that many [Indians] were killed and others were captured and defeated." Columbus sent hundreds of Native Americans to Spain as slaves, because he still had not found enough gold to make his colony valuable to Ferdinand and Isabella.

By 1496, Columbus knew that the Spanish rulers had heard of his problems on Hispaniola. He returned to Spain, hoping to convince them he was still a hero.

Before Christopher Columbus, Italians never ate their spaghetti covered in tomato sauce, and Native Americans never rode horses across the Great Plains. With his explorations, Columbus started a two-way trade of goods between Europe and the Americas that continued for centuries. In this "Columbian Exchange," Europeans discovered plants and animals they never knew existed, as Columbus brought samples of what he found back to Europe. In return, he and other Europeans brought new animals and foods to the Western Hemisphere.

Those who explored the Americas brought the first potatoes, tomatoes, corn, and several kinds of beans back to Europe. Later, some of these crops were also introduced to Africa and Asia. The Spanish brought such crops as wheat, rice, coffee, and bananas to the Americas.

The Columbian Exchange was not always helpful, however. The Spanish brought new, deadly diseases from Europe to the Americas. **Smallpox,** for example, killed countless Native Americans. Other illnesses carried to the Americas included tuberculosis, a lung disease, and measles.

Chapter Four

Last Voyages

Ships leave the harbor at Cadiz, Spain, on May 3, 1992, on a voyage commemorating the 500th anniversary of Columbus's historic first voyage to the Americas.

Sailing on the *Niña,* Columbus reached Cadiz, Spain, in June 1496. Ferdinand and Isabella did not seem to welcome him as joyfully as they had in 1493. Columbus spent almost two years trying to convince them to back a third trip to the Americas. Finally, in May 1498, he left Spain. This time, he had only six ships, and three of them were carrying supplies for the colonists at Hispaniola. Columbus took the other three ships to continue his exploration of the Americas.

This third voyage was short, but important. Columbus landed on the mainland of South America, in what is now Venezuela. He became the first European to land on the main landmass of the Western Hemisphere since the Norse explorer Leif Eriksson. Columbus later wrote, "I have come to believe that this is a mighty continent which was hitherto unknown. . . . And if this is a continent it is a wonderful thing and will be so regarded by all men of learning." Columbus later told Ferdinand and Isabella that he had found Paradise, the place where good Christians believed they would go after they died. The explorer thought he had gone beyond Asia to reach this incredible place.

Leaving South America, Columbus sailed for Hispaniola. His brothers Bartolomeo and Diego, who ruled while he was gone, were having a hard time dealing with the Native Americans and unhappy colonists. The situation improved slightly at the end of 1499, when the settlers found a large gold mine on the island. But the next year, Columbus was trying to end a rebellion against him. By that time, Ferdinand and Isabella had decided to replace him as the viceroy of Hispaniola.

In August 1500, Francisco de Bobadilla arrived from Spain to take that position. He saw that Columbus and

Columbus spent time in prison when he was sent back to Spain in 1500. When he was finally able to see Queen Isabella and King Ferdinand, he was released.

his brothers had killed some of the rebels. Bobadilla also heard about other crimes the Italians might have committed. The new viceroy arrested Columbus and sent him back to Spain. This time, Columbus crossed the Atlantic tied up in chains.

A Sad End

Back in Spain, Columbus spent about five weeks in jail before he could see Ferdinand and Isabella. The Spanish rulers were sorry Columbus had been jailed. Although he had failed as viceroy, they still respected him and his deeds—especially acquiring new lands for Spain.

Columbus wanted to make sure the rulers gave him all the money and government positions they had promised him. He wrote a book defending his claim to the riches he was supposed to receive. In another book, Columbus wrote that God had chosen him to find the Americas and spread Christianity. One historian has called this book "bizarre," and there is no proof Ferdinand and Isabella ever read it. Still, it shows how much religion shaped Columbus's explorations.

By now, Columbus had shown he could be demanding, unreasonable, and perhaps a bit greedy. Still, the Spanish rulers agreed to back one more voyage to the Americas. They also told him not to return to Hispaniola. Columbus, however, defied that order. In the summer of 1502, he reached the island with four caravels. As a storm approached, he asked the

Columbus shows a map of the Americas to Ferdinand and Isabella. Each time he wanted to make a new voyage to the Americas, he had to convince the king and queen to provide financial support.

colonists to let his ships land. The Spaniards refused, and Columbus sailed on. He explored the coast of Central America and once again sought new sources of gold. He also looked for—but never found—a **strait** that would lead his ships to Asia.

By June 1503, with just two damaged ships still under his command, Columbus landed on Jamaica. The ships could not be fixed, and he sent some men in canoes to Hispaniola to seek help. He was sick, as he had often been during the past few years. In a letter he wrote to Ferdinand and Isabella, Columbus said, "My body is infirm and exhausted. . . . I have wept for others; now have pity on me." Columbus waited in Jamaica for a year before his men returned with a rescue ship.

After a brief stay on Hispaniola, the great explorer returned to Spain for the last time. Shortly after Columbus returned, Isabella died. Of the two royal rulers, she had always been closest to him. Her husband, Ferdinand, waited months before meeting with Columbus, and the king refused to give him the extra money he wanted for his discoveries. Still, Columbus had made a small fortune from his efforts—although not as much as he thought he deserved.

During the next year, Columbus's health worsened. On May 20, 1506, he died in Valladolid, Spain. The Spanish public did not hear about his death for 10 years. By then, other European explorers had sailed to new lands. For hundreds of years, many more would cross the oceans, seeking wealth and fame. None, however, would ever match the deeds of a single brave, determined sailor named Christopher Columbus.

Christopher Columbus was just the first of many great explorers who sailed for Spain. A member of Columbus's second voyage, Juan Ponce de León, won fame as the leader of his own expedition. Sailing from Puerto Rico in 1513, Ponce de León explored southern Florida. The same year, Vasco Nuñez de Balboa won fame as the first European to see the Pacific Ocean. On his last voyage, Columbus had sailed to within just 40 miles (64 km) of the Pacific when he reached the eastern coast of Panama.

Other great Spanish explorers traveled across the continents of the Americas. Hernando Cortés led his troops through Central America, taking control of an empire ruled by the Aztecs. In South America, Francisco Pizarro (above) explored and won lands that belonged to another great Native American people, the Incas. And during the 1530s and 1540s, such explorers as Francisco Vásquez de Coronado, Hernando de Soto, and Álvar Nuñez Cabeza de Vaca traveled through large parts of what is now the southern United States. One hundred years after Columbus first sailed, Spain controlled the largest overseas empire in the world.

1451: Christopher Columbus is born in Genoa, Italy.

1465: Columbus sails for the first time.

1476: According to Hernando Columbus, his father was ship-wrecked this year off the coast of Portugal, but no other proof exists of this incident.

1477: After a brief stay in Lisbon, Portugal, Columbus sails to England and Iceland.

1484: King John II of Portugal refuses to back Columbus's plan to sail west to the Indies, in Asia.

1486: Columbus meets King Ferdinand and Queen Isabella of Spain. They appoint a group of scholars to study the plan for his voyage.

1492: Spain defeats the Moors. Ferdinand and Isabella finally agree to pay for Columbus's voyage to the Indies. In August, Columbus sails with three ships to the Canary Islands, then heads for the Indies. In October, Columbus lands in the Bahamas and names the first island he finds San Salvador. He meets the native people of the region, the Taínos. In November, Martín Pinzón, captain of the *Pinta,* sails off on his own. He later rejoins the expedition. In December, Columbus lands at Hispaniola. Later in the month, the *Santa María* is destroyed.

1493: In January, Columbus leaves 39 men at La Navidad, Hispaniola, and returns to Spain with his remaining two ships. In March, the expedition returns to Spain and Columbus is greeted as a hero. In September, Columbus returns to the Americas to start a colony on Hispaniola. In November, reaching La Navidad, Columbus finds that the sailors he left behind have been killed.

1494: Columbus begins a new settlement in Hispaniola and uses the Taínos as slaves. He faces problems with some of the Spanish settlers who do not want to follow his orders.

1496: Columbus returns to Spain.

1498: In May, Columbus begins his third voyage west, reaching the Americas in July. He then explores the coast of South America and comes ashore at what is now Venezuela.

1500: Francisco de Bobadilla, the new viceroy of Hispaniola, arrests Columbus for his treatment of some of the Spanish settlers. Columbus returns to Spain in chains.

1502: In April, Columbus sails on his fourth and last voyage to the Americas. He explores the coast of Central America.

1503: His ships damaged, Columbus lands at Jamaica and sends some of his crew in a canoe to seek help from the settlers at Hispaniola.

1504: Columbus and his sailors are rescued and return to Spain.

1506: On May 20, Columbus dies at his home in Valladolid, Spain.

cartographer (kar-TOG-ruh-fuhr) A cartographer is a person who makes maps. Bartolomeo Columbus was working as a cartographer in Portugal when his brother Christopher began planning his voyage of exploration.

converted (kuhn-VURT-ed) People who give up one set of religious beliefs for another have converted. In Columbus's time, many Jews living in Spain converted to Christianity.

expedition (ek-spuh-DISH-uhn) An expedition is a major journey made for a special reason, such as to explore new lands. Columbus led an expedition across the Atlantic Ocean for Spain.

Moors (MORS) The Moors were North Africans who followed the Islamic religion. They had conquered large portions of Spain. In 1492, Ferdinand and Isabella won back the last Spanish lands that had been ruled by the Moors.

mutiny (MYOO-tih-nee) A mutiny is a plan to overthrow a leader, especially the captain of a ship. Some of the crew on Columbus's ship started to plan a mutiny.

Norse (NORSS) Norse refers to people from Norway who settled Iceland, Greenland, and parts of northern Europe more than 1,000 years ago. The Norse explorer Leif Eriksson was the first European known to have reached North America.

rudder (RUHD-ur) A rudder is a mechanism that helps steer a ship. The rudder of one of Columbus's ships was damaged on his first voyage west.

smallpox (SMAWL-poks) Smallpox is a disease that spreads easily and causes chills, fever, and a rash. Smallpox killed many Native Americans who had never been exposed to it before Columbus arrived in the Americas.

strait (STRAYT) A strait is a narrow water passage that connects two larger bodies of water. Columbus hoped to find a strait in South America that connected the Atlantic and Pacific Oceans.

viceroy (VISSE-roi) A viceroy rules in place of a king in a distant land. Ferdinand and Isabella of Spain named Columbus their viceroy in the lands he found in the Americas.

Books

Aller, Susan Bivin. *Christopher Columbus.* Minneapolis: Lerner Publications, 2003.

Alter, Judy. *Christopher Columbus: Explorer.* Chanhasssen, Minn.: The Child's World, 2002.

Gallagher, Carole S. *Christopher Columbus and the Discovery of the New World.* Philadelphia: Chelsea House Publishers, 2000.

Jacobs, Francine. *The Taínos: The People Who Welcomed Columbus.* New York: G. P. Putnams's Sons, 1992.

Sundel, Al. *Christopher Columbus and the Age of Exploration in World History.* Berkeley Heights, N.J.: Enslow Publishers, 2002.

Web Sites

Visit our Web page for lots of links about Christopher Columbus:
http://www.childsworld.com/links.html

Note to parents, teachers, and librarians: We routinely check our Web links to make sure they're safe, active sites—so encourage your readers to check them out!

About the Author

Michael Burgan is a freelance writer of books for children and adults. A history graduate of the University of Connecticut, he has written more than 60 fiction and nonfiction children's books for various publishers. For adult audiences, he has written news articles, essays, and plays. Michael Burgan is a recipient of an Edpress Award and belongs to the Society of Children's Book Writers and Illustrators.

Index

Arawak Indians, 21
Aztec empire, 35

Balboa, Vasco Nuñez de, 35
Barcelona, Spain, 26
Bobadilla, Francisco de, 31–32

caciques (Taíno chiefs), 21
Cadiz, Spain, 30, *30*
Canary Islands, 17, *18*
Christianity, 16, 22, 31, 32
Columbian Exchange, 29
Columbus, Bartolomeo (brother), 12,
  31
Columbus, Christopher, 7, *8, 9, 11,
  15, 16, 24, 32, 33*
  arrest, 32, *32*
  birth, 11
  death, *7,* 34
  education, 11–12
  physical description, 10
  as viceroy, 16
Columbus, Diego (brother), 31
Columbus, Hernando (son), 10
Coronado, Francisco Vásquez de, 35
Cortés, Hernando, 35

Eriksson, Leif, 13, *13,* 31

Ferdinand, king of Spain, 14, 15, 16,
  16, 26, 28, 30, 31, 32, *33,* 34

Genoa, Italy, 11, 12
gold, 7, 22–23, 26, 28, 31, 33

Hispaniola, 24, 25, 27, 28, 33, 34

Inca empire, 35
La Isabela settlement, 28
Isabella, queen of Spain, 14, 15, 16,
  16, 26, 28, 30, 31, 32, *33,* 34

Jamaica, 33, 34
John II, king of Portugal, 14, 25, 26

Lisbon, Portugal, 12, 25–26

Moors, 15, 16

Native Americans, 6, 9, 20, 21, *21,*
  22, *24,* 27, *27,* 28, 29, *29,* 31, 35
La Navidad settlement, 25, 27
Newfoundland, Canada, 13
Niña (ship), 17, 24–25, 30
Norse exploration, 13, *13,* 31

Pinta (ship), 17, 19, 23, 25
Pinzón, Martín Alonso, 17, 18, 19,
  23–24, *23*
Pinzón, Vicente Yañez, 17
Pizarro, Francisco, 35, *35*
Ponce de León, Juan, 35
Portugal, 12, 14, 15

San Salvador, 20
Santa María (flagship), 17, 24
settlers, 26, *27,* 31
slavery, 9, 28
Soto, Hernando de, 35
Spain, 8, 15, 26, 28, 30, *30,* 35

Taíno Indians, 21, 22, 27, *27*

Vaca, Álvar Nuñez Cabeza de, 35
Valladolid, Spain, 34